THE TEMPLE KING SOLOMON BUILT

I KINGS 5 FOR CHILDREN

Written by Joanne M. Bates
Illustrated by Bill Heuer

ARCH Books

Copyright © 1982 CONCORDIA PUBLISHING HOUSE

ST. LOUIS, MISSOURI

MANUFACTURED IN THE UNITED STATES OF AMERICA

ALL RIGHTS RESERVED

ISBN 0-570-06155-5

King David had a lot of sons,
He loved them every one;
Young Solomon grew up secure
With school and games and fun.

He knew that someday he would sit
Upon his father's throne;
He did his best to learn about
The jobs that must be done.

"Tell me again," he'd ask his dad,
"About your plans to build
A house to worship our great God
On Araunah's threshing-floor field."

"Yes, Son," the king would say,
"For there an angel paused,
When God, in mercy, stopped the plague
My selfishness had caused.

"I said to Nathan,
God's prophet, 'Now see—
I like my new palace.
It suits my family.

" 'But in a tent
God's ark has been;
It should have a new house—
Fancy, like mine.' "

"What is the ark?" asked Solomon,
"The big boat where Noah did ride?"
"No! It's the box Moses made long ago
To keep the Ten Commandments inside."

"But I must not build it;
I've fought long hard wars.
Nathan heard God say
That task would be yours.

"So look in the storerooms
At all I am saving,
Of silver and bronze,
And gold for your having."

When David grew too old to reign,
He said, "Now you are king;
You'll have my throne and chariot,
You'll wear my royal ring."

The new king went to Gibeon
To seek God's guidance there,
And near the big bronze altar
He offered up a prayer.

God talked to Solomon that night.
Saying, "What can I give to you?"
Thinking about all the people he'd lead,
He asked to be good, wise, and true.

Because he was humble,
God granted his wishes;
King Solomon had power,
Fame, wisdom, and riches.

No other king has even been
So great and wise as he;
He told of plants and animals,
Of fishes in the sea.

Writing a song was easy for him,
Proverbs God brought into mind.
When asked to decide about matters of law,
Solomon was both fair and kind.

At last he was ready
The temple to start.
The people of Israel
Were glad to take part,

Two months at home,
Then one month in Lebanon,
Cutting the fir trees
And cedar to float down.

King Hiram of Tyre
Gladly sold them the wood;
He sent his own servants
To help as they could.

Foreigners were picked to carry
Burdens to and from the boats;
Others cut stones from the mountains,
Frightening deer and billy goats.

No banging, clanging noises bothered
Workers at the building site;
They simply put together pieces
Other men had cut just right.

First foundations, deep and sturdy,
Then the walls reached to the sky;
Ceilings, narrow windows, pillars,
Gold and jewels placed low and high.

In the "Holy of Holies" room
Where God's ark soon would be,
Gold-covered angel statues stood
Spreading their wings protectively.

Golden lampstands held the candles;
A special table held showbread.
Sacrifices would be on the altar
As the laws of God had said.

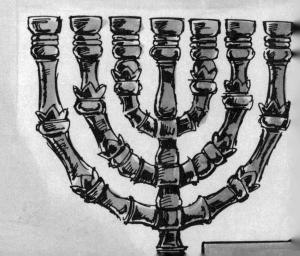

For seven years the work progressed
On Mount Moriah it was done,
Till Solomon's grand and glorious temple—
FINISHED!
Glistened in the evening sun.

The Israelites came joyfully
To dedicate God's house;
On a stage so all could see,
King Solomon knelt reverently.

He prayed for God above to bless
The temple, folks, and land;
He prayed for mercy from the Lord,
He prayed with outstretched hand.

Then suddenly a heavenly fire
Burned sacrifices there;
God's glory—a bright cloud—came down!
The Lord had heard the prayer.

How happy were the celebrants!
They had a great big feast;
For seven days they all rejoiced—
People, king, and priest.

The temple showed God's holiness,
His presence, watchful eye.
For all who trust and will obey,
God *still* is waiting nigh.

DEAR PARENTS:

In the Old Testament the temple was the symbol of God's abiding presence with His covenant people. He lived with them, forgiving their sins, supplying their needs, and empowering them to meet their challenges.

We need to know that God lives with us, too. He is present with us not as a powerful ruler or lawgiver, but as a loving Father, One who sent His Son to be our Brother and to suffer and die in our place. When we hear how our sins are forgiven in Jesus Christ, or when we're reminded how we actually rose from the dead with Jesus in Baptism (Romans 6:3-4), we realize how God *is* with us in a very special way through these means of grace.

Help your children see what it means to have their loving heavenly Father present with them always. He faithfully protected and delivered His children in the Old Testament. He promises to do no less for us today.

THE EDITOR